body & soul

body & soul

Created by Judith Thompson
with fifteen women

Playwrights Canada Press

Toronto

PLAYWRIGHTS CANADA PRESS
The Canadian Drama Publisher
215 Spadina Ave., Suite 230, Toronto, ON Canada M5T 2C7
phone 416.703.0013 fax 416.408.3402
orders@playwrightscanada.com • www.playwrightscanada.com

Playwrights Canada Press acknowledges the financial support of the Government of Canada
through the Canada Book Fund and the Canada Council for the Arts and the Province of
Ontario through the Ontario Arts Council and the Ontario Media Development Corporation
for our publishing activities.

Cover image © Rita Leistner
Cover and type design by Blake Sproule

LIBRARY AND ARCHIVES CANADA CATALOGUING IN PUBLICATION

Thompson, Judith, 1954-
Body & soul / created by Judith Thompson with fifteen women.

ISBN 978-0-88754-895-6

I. Title. II. Title: Body and soul.

PS8589.H527B63 2010   C812'.54   C2010-906543-3

First edition: January 2011
Printed and bound in Canada by Solisco - Tri-Graphic, Ottawa

I would like to dedicate this play to our great-great-grandmothers, watching us from wherever they may be.

Foreword

One day last February Judith Thompson phoned to tell me about her third production of *Body & Soul*, which was to be part of the Cultural Olympiad in Vancouver in March. Her oldest cast member was unable to continue due to ill health. Judith asked me if I could take her place. Without a moment's hesitation I said "YES!" I was free, I was a huge admirer of Judith's writing, and I had wanted to work with her again since we had shared the stage in Kingston when she was eleven years old.

Judith explained that I would be working with twelve women, all non-professional actors and I would be telling my own life stories. I had been working in professional theatre for forty odd years and always with a playwright's script, so this would be a unique and rather daunting experience!

Prior to the two-week rehearsal period in Toronto, Maria Costa, the stage manager, sent me DVDs of the 2008 production of *Body & Soul*. This was wonderful as it gave me an overview of the set, the format, and the women and their stories. I was so impressed with their confidence, their courage, and the immediate connection they made with the audience. The audience stood and applauded at the end and so did I.

I was looking forward to the work, but first I had to write my own life stories. This was difficult and challenging; it meant metaphorically baring the "body and soul," writing honestly about memories both painful and comical for Judith to edit. I don't know what I expected from the rehearsal process but what I received was the warm welcome of twelve amazing women and their riveting, moving, and often hilarious life stories; and the inspired and inspiring direction of Judith who deftly moulded the stories into a whole.

My "unique and daunting experience" turned into the joyful and fulfilling run in Vancouver with its sold-out performances, cheers, and standing ovations. I will never forget the woman who told us after the show, "I am so grateful, your stories have changed my life," and the man who said, "Thank you for the insight you have given me into the women in my life."

Thank *you* Judith.

—Carolyn Hetherington, September 2010

Preface

BRENDA SURMINSKI, OF OGILVY & MATHER, ADVERTISERS FOR DOVE
Would you be interested in writing a play about beauty and aging, using real women over the age of forty-five as performers?

JUDITH   Real women?

BRENDA   Ordinary women, not professional actresses or performers.

JUDITH   Oh. Um… I must tell you, I know many actresses and most of them are actually real women.

BRENDA   Oh yes, of course, but their bread and butter relies on them being as physically close to Hollywood perfect as possible. We want to show people that every woman is beautiful, that aging is not something to be dreaded. That it can be the best time of a woman's life.

JUDITH   Okay, sure, I mean, I am fifty-two and… better than ever. Fatter than ever, but better than ever. In my opinion.

BRENDA   I think a theatre piece about this could be very, very interesting.

JUDITH   Are you okay with using real women then?

BRENDA   Absolutely.

JUDITH   I'm fifty-two, it's all about artistic adventure. As long as…

BRENDA	As long as...
JUDITH	No advertising. Of any kind.
BRENDA	Of course not.
JUDITH	No promotion of Dove products in the play.
BRENDA	Absolutely not.
JUDITH	There will be no talk of products of any kind.
BRENDA	Fine!
JUDITH	And... although the central idea will be these women are stronger and better than ever, I am not going to shy away from any truths. If they have been through hell, if they are going through hell, we are going to hear about it.
BRENDA	No problem. GREAT. What do you need?
JUDITH	Absolute arms-length trust.

They gave me everything I needed. YES, even autonomy. We all agree that, generally, as soon as an artist accepts the money of a corporation, there is a serious danger that the artist will lose her voice, she will be strangled, because, the theory is, artists are all about subversion, not compliance.

But the difference here is that the extraordinary women at Ogilvy & Mather, especially Brenda Surminski, and even the amazing Unilever folks, Sharon MacLeod and Margaret McKellar, wanted to support subversion. It was subversion to even say pro-age instead of anti-age, and especially to showcase the voices, the stories of middle-aged and elderly women, women who were not Queens, or CEOs, or movie stars. Ordinary, mostly post-fertile women. Women who generally are invisible, and unheard.

This was an act of revolution and I was very glad to be part of it.

So we began by asking women all over Canada who were interested in appearing in a play about beauty and aging to write a letter to their body and to send us a picture with their particulars.

We received thousands of letters from all over the country. Funny, intelligent, sometimes not so intelligent, poignant, sad, reflective, unique, sometimes clichéd, but always from the heart.

By this time I had hired Iris Nemani, the brilliant artistic producer who had been the general manager of Nightwood Theatre, and who had worked with me over several years to produce Shakespeare with sixty to seventy kids in grades four to six at Palmerston Public School in Toronto.

Diversity was of prime importance to me, I wanted to hear from women of different backgrounds. I was dismayed by whiteness on our stages. These women were going to be a mosaic of our country, of our history, and history is written in the body.

Iris and I, with the help of Jigsaw Casting, whittled the submissions down to about forty.

We held day-long auditions in which I asked the women to talk about something they were passionate about. I gave them trigger words, such as mother, children, regret, ugly, old, and hate. I met with them individually because it was critical that the chemistry was right. I asked them to bring a poem in and eighty percent of them brought Maya Angelou's "Phenomenal Woman," a wonderful poem, but it was amusing to hear it read over and over... I asked them to participate in an improvisation with several others to see how they worked in an ensemble situation.

It was not easy choosing fifteen performers out of the wonderful forty women who auditioned, but amazingly, we all agreed in the end.

In May 2007, we had our first two-week workshop; we began by reciting all the female names in our families as far back as we could go. Most of us couldn't go farther back than our grandmothers, which was telling. Women are easily forgotten.

I began to devise a possible structure, and would build the workshop day around an idea, such as "earliest childhood memories" or "most erotic moments" or "how would you describe your present state of being in one word or phrase"; i.e. "I'm Rhonda, I'm forty-nine, and I'm waiting for something, but don't think for a minute it's true love" or "I'm Barbie, I'm fifty-four and I'm restless." Regrets. Children. Lovers. Body. Compliments, insults, and probably the section I am most proud of: the moment when each of them knew they were finally a woman. I didn't feel that this section was perfect until the final production at the Cultural Olympiad in Vancouver, March 2010. We heard hundreds and hundreds of accounts of "when I finally felt I was a woman"—this section was definitely the most challenging, but when the story was finally right, it was like lightning striking—this section electrified the end of the first act.

Though some of the stories went through many versions, some were perfect the first time and have never been changed since that first workshop, such as Gloria's story about the bus trip she and her sister took from Brooklyn to Landis, North Carolina. Not a word was changed in that story. Others needed to be heavily edited, and many were too private to ever be told in public. I pushed very hard, asking the women for more, another story, a better story, more interesting details, more honesty, and astonishingly, they all eventually found their strongest story.

I don't think I could do what these women did. I suppose that is why I am a playwright, I tell my story in an elliptical and deeply hidden way through characters who are wildly different from me and from everyone I know I learned so much about courage and authenticity from these women. When they were speaking in their own unique voices, with details only they could remember, the stories worked. Whenever they veered into cliché, or over-explaining, or interpreting, the stories stopped working.

I don't know what to call this play. Certainly NOT a play authored by Judith Thompson, but not exactly a collective in the usual sense either. Most of the performers are very powerful writers, though they are not playwrights. If any reader has an idea for a short and snappy category title, please, send it our way. My hope is that those who are inspired by these stories will be unafraid to open their mouths and tell their own stories, confident in the knowledge that these are stories the world is waiting to hear.

—Judith Thompson, September 2010

A Note from Dove

Dove believes beauty has no age limit. And now, we have a play to prove it.

Too many people believe beauty has an age limit. Too many believe aging is something to be avoided at all costs. Too many believe that becoming older and becoming invisible go hand in hand.

Dove believes it's time for all these age-old attitudes toward women to change. So we commissioned Judith Thompson, a playwright whose work is synonymous with generating controversy, to create *Body & Soul*, a provocative new play that challenges the way society thinks about beauty and aging.

Through a cast of fifteen real women with no previous acting experience, our collective creation will act as a seed for societal change.

Why a play? Because we believe nothing speaks louder or more passionately when it comes to inciting dialogue and overturning the status quo. Also, we hope some of you might be inspired to play a more active role by staging your own production of *Body & Soul* within your community.

Our wish is that you open these pages with the desire to read a beautiful play. And that you are left with the desire, in one way or another, to help us ignite a beautiful revolution.

Body & Soul was first performed at the Young Centre in Toronto, Ontario, on May 10, 2008, with the following cast and crew:

Jeannine Boucher
Polly (Ramkissoon) Clarke
Lois Fine
Francine Robert-Grainger
Ann Marie Hasley
Glenda Klassen
Janice Kulyk Keefer
Barbara Nichol
Pauline Patten
Ruth Rakoff
Gloria Schmed-Scott
Rhonda Tepper
Judy Wark

Playwright/Director	Judith Thompson
Producer	Iris Nemani
Set Designer	Sue Le Page
Lighting/Projection Designer	Magi Oman
Costume Designer	Dana Osborne
Sound Design/Composer	Cathy Nosaty
Movement Coordinator	Sarah Dempsey
Stage Manager	Maria Costa
Apprentice Stage Manager	Sandi Becker
Dramaturge	Iris Turcott

Body & Soul was also performed at the Tarragon Extra Space in Toronto, Ontario, on June 4, 2009, with the following cast and crew:

Joanna Anaquod
Jeannine Boucher
Polly (Ramkissoon) Clarke
Lois Fine
Francine Robert-Grainger
Ann Marie Hasley
Janice Kulyk Keefer
Barbara Nichol
Pauline Patten
Ruth Rakoff
Gloria Schmed-Scott
Rhonda Tepper

Playwright/Director	Judith Thompson
Producers	Judith Thompson
	Lois Fine
	Barbara Nichol
	Brenda Surminski
	Maria Costa
	Gloria Schmed-Scott
	Francine Robert -Grainger
Set Designer	Sue Le Page
Costume Designer	Dana Osborne
Composer	Cathy Nosaty
Stage Manager	Maria Costa
Lighting Designer	Jennifer Jimenez
Assistant Lighting Designer	Kai Yueh Chen

Body & Soul was also performed at the Firehall Arts Centre as part of the Cultural Olympiad, Vancouver 2010, on March 11, 2010, with the following cast and crew:

Polly (Ramkissoon) Clarke
Lois Fine
Francine Robert-Grainger
Ann Marie Hasley
Carolyn Hetherington
Glenda Klassen
Janice Kulyk Keefer
Barbara Nichol
Pauline Patten
Ruth Rakoff
Gloria Schmed-Scott
Rhonda Tepper
Judy Wark

Playwright/Director	Judith Thompson
Producers	Judith Thompson
	Lois Fine
	Brenda Surminski
	Maria Costa
Set Designer	Sue Le Page
Costume Designer	Dana Osborne
Composer	Cathy Nosaty
Stage Manager	Maria Costa
Lighting Designer	Jennifer Jimenez
Assistant Lighting Designer	Kai Yueh Chen

The Women

Joanna
Jeannine
Polly
Lois
Francine
Ann Marie
Carolyn
Glenda
Janice
Barbie
Pauline
Ruth
Gloria
Rhonda
Judy

Act One

Walking Women

Lights to black, except for a live musician, if possible. The lights brighten to a dusky look, and one of the women walks to the middle and pauses. Others come out, in twos, threes, and sometimes alone. They walk quickly, slowly, as if waking from a dream. Then there is a moment when the music changes and the lights brighten and they see each other. They feel secure, at home, and spend the next minute or so finding their place on the stage. When everybody is in place, the music stops and the words begin. This should take about three to five minutes.

JANICE   I'm Janice, I'm fifty-seven, and I'm as curious as ever.

RUTH   I'm Ruth. I'm a renewed and recycled forty-seven.

POLLY   I'm Polly. I'm sixty-five and I really truly believe in karma.

GLENDA   I'm Glenda, I'm fifty-five, and I'm released.

JUDY   I'm Judy, I'm fifty-four and I *finally* know that I can make it on my own.

ANN MARIE   I'm Ann Marie Anastasia. I'm forty-nine and I am flying.

BARBIE   I'm Barbie. I'm fifty-five, and I'm restless.

LOIS   I'm Lois. I'm fifty-one. I'm a worrier and a warrior.

PAULINE   I'm Pauline. I'm fifty-eight. I'm proud and peppery.

JOANNA   I am Joanna. I'm fifty-three, Soto First Nations, and I am ridiculously happy.

FRANCINE   My name is Francine. I am sixty-three. Je suis Francine, j'ai soixante-trois ans. Je suis bien ici, maintenant, avec vous.

GLORIA   I'm Gloria. I'm sixty-five and I have a secret.

RHONDA   I'm Rhonda. I'm fifty. I'm waiting for something and don't assume for a minute it's true love.

CAROLYN   I'm Carolyn, I'm almost seventy-nine years old and I can hear the beating of wings.

JEANNINE   Je m'appelle Jeannine and je suis a surprised seventy-nine. Every day is a gratification.

The women move to a semicircle around CAROLYN *and* JEANNINE.

ALL   Vive la Reine-Mère!

Intros

The women stand in a straight line downstage.

JANICE   I was found in a field and born without a face.

RUTH   I compulsively sculpted dozens of tiny breasts and gave them away.

POLLY   My secret Hindu name is Lakpati, which means a thousand lovers; it was a gift, and a curse: because of love, I lost my greatest love.

GLENDA   Tansi. I am Cree First Nation. For many years I abandoned myself.

JUDY   My husband Andrew died of melanoma at thirty-eight. He left me with three young children.

ANN MARIE When I was growing up I was called "Tall Twelve," "Giraffe," and "Skinny Bitch," but I never had my mother around to comfort me.

BARBIE   Both my poor grandfathers killed themselves. I thought when other children had grandfathers they just hadn't done it yet.

LOIS   About twenty years ago, I almost lost my beloved son because I am not his biological mother.

PAULINE   Growing up in Jamaica, I had no shoes at all and I was beaten for breathing.

JOANNA   I was born into racism. I became a racist.

FRANCINE Why did you? How could you? Do you ever think about it? 'Cause I do.

GLORIA   I endured police brutality, insults, water hoses, and jail.

RHONDA   At the age of six, I began to lose my hearing and by the time I was eighteen I was profoundly deaf.

CAROLYN   Sixteen years ago I was onstage playing Daisy in *Driving Miss Daisy* when I had a hemorrhagic stroke—bleeding in the brain.

JEANNINE 1929. The Crash. I was born into fear.

          The women turn toward stage right and walk back to the structures, remaining in a straight line with their backs to the audience. BARBIE *stays downstage and addresses the audience for "The Lady in the Mirror."*

3

The Lady in the Mirror

She begins after inspecting herself in an imaginary mirror.

BARBIE   That lady in that mirror
She really isn't me
We used to look the same but
We're different now, you see.

The fact is she's aging
At quite a rapid pace.
And time has left its claw marks,
On a her once *quite pleasant* face.

Oh, there is some resemblance
This minor point I'll grant
On certain days in certain ways
She does look just like my aunt.

And I'm not superficial
I loved my auntie well.
She kept an *inner* beauty
As her looks went straight to hell.

Gesturing toward mirror.

Now that thing might have troubles
Or too much on her plate.
She's getting up too early,
She's staying up too late.

Or maybe it's the lighting
That's crucial, you'll agree.
Or it could be her outfit
(Which looks okay on me).

There's *one* thing that gives me pause
Just how can it be true?
That I don't age but, Jesus,
(into audience) Look at what life has done to you.

Mothers' Names

By the end of "The Lady in the Mirror," the women have formed two horizontal lines downstage. As each woman speaks, she raises her arms.

JANICE   Natalya. Olena. Domicella. Melania.

RUTH   Genesha. Birtha. Betty. Gina.

POLLY   Tilcoarie. Mahadaye. Mary Jankey. Lakpatiya.

GLENDA   Celina Rose. Patricia Eva Ernestine.

JUDY   Alice. Agnes. Audrey. Wong See.

ANN MARIE   Molly. Cynthia. Cita. Winifred.

BARBIE   Sally. Marjorie. Marjorie. Marjorie. Marjorie Elizabeth.

LOIS   Joy. Sybil. Ann. Raisel.

PAULINE   Urith.

JOANNA   Sophia. Eva. Jane. Amelia. Sarah Anne.

FRANCINE   Delia. Maria. Fernande.

GLORIA   Mary Magdeleine. Mary Naomi. Martha. LouLou.

RHONDA   Evelyn. Shirley. Mary. Leva.

CAROLYN   Gwendolyn. Elise. Anna. Evelyn. Irene.

JEANNINE   Hermine. Pamela. Marianne.

All the women lower their arms and stay in position.

Childhood Songs

JANICE sings, walking around the women.

JANICE   *(Ukrainian song)* Toschi toschi…

RUTH sings and walks around the women.

RUTH   *(Hebrew song)* Abba bah… Sababa…

POLLY dances in a circle as she sings "Rosie Gal." Both the dance and song are repeated by the others.

POLLY   Ay, Rosie gal what you cookin' for dinner? Every time I pass you, you grinding masala…

ALL   Ay, Rosie gal what you cookin' for dinner? Every time I pass you, you grinding masala…

The women sit.

FRANCINE   1, 2, 3, 4, 5, 6, 7, Violette! Violette!
1, 2, 3, 4, 5, 6, 7, Violette à bicyclette!

CAROLYN   I wish I was an owl's egg
Sitting in a tree—
Doing nothing all day long
Just sitting there you see—
And then a little boy would come
And gaze on me with glee—
And then I'd bust my little self
And cover him with me

GLORIA stands and claps along to her song.

GLENDA   Tipihkan, (It is night)
Tipihkan, Ninipeyin, (I will put you to sleep)
Pakanishi Kikapawa'atam (You will dream of another place)
Minonipan (Sleep peacefully).

GLORIA   I am a pretty little black girl,

As pretty as pretty can be,
And all the boys around my block they come and play,
With me me!
My boyfriend's name is Black Sambo,
He comes from Alabambo,
With a cherry on his toes and
A boogie in his nose,
And that's the way
My story goes.

PAULINE stands atop the structure stage left, singing a traditional Jamaican children's song.

PAULINE A chi chi bud ho!
Suma them a halla suma ball
Suma black bird
Suma dem a halla suma ball
Suma chick chick
Suma dem a halla suma ball
A chi chi bud ho!

ALL Suma dem a halla suma ball

PAULINE Suma chick chick

ALL Suma dem a halla suma ball

BARBIE When my sisters and I were small, we would chant to get our father to come to say good night. So from three little bedrooms, three little voices would sing: "Daddy, daddy, daddy, daddy oh, Daddy. Daddy, daddy daddy daddy, oh."

JUDY rises.

JUDY This is a lullaby Andrew taught my little girl, Gracie, when he was dying:

My pigeon house I open wide
and I set all my pigeons free.
They fly all around way up, way down
and they sit on the tallest tree

And when they return
from their merry merry flight
I close the door and I say good night
Coocooroo coocooroo coocooroo
coocooroo coocooroo coocooroo
cooroo...

        RHONDA gets up. She sings and signs "Row, Row, Row Your Boat."

RHONDA   Row, row, row your boat
Gently down the stream
Merrily, merrily, merrily, merrily
Life is but a dream.

        ALL sign "Row, Row, Row" for one bar.

        LOIS stands and stomps around the women.

LOIS   Lois Fine is no good, chop her into firewood! When she's dead jump on her head and make her into gingerbread!

ALL   *(stomping with LOIS as they make their way to the structure)* Lois Fine is no good, chop her into firewood! When she's dead jump on her head and make her into gingerbread!

Childhood Stories

        The women sit and stand around the structure, except JANICE who sits downstage on a stool. Each woman will take her spot either downstage or on the stool as she tells her childhood story.

JANICE   We had just moved to a new suburb where's everybody's name was Jones or Brown or McGregor. One of our new neighbours had come over to meet my mother; when she heard that our name was Kulyk, she said, "I thought people with names like yours cleaned the houses of people with names like mine." So it was no small thing when a girl from school asked me back to her house to play. We walked into the kitchen and the girl, whom I didn't know very well, put out cookies on a plate. I wasn't hungry but it was only when she was pouring out two tall glasses of milk that I knew how badly I had to pee. I couldn't ask where the bathroom was—she would know I meant "toilet" and the word suddenly seemed like something dirty. And so I drank down my milk as the pee trickled down my leg (JANICE *slowly pours out a glass of water into a bowl that has been set down beside her stool.*) onto linoleum. The girl started to snicker as she threw me a rag to mop up with. She smiled, and I knew that she would always have power over me. And as I wiped my pee off her kitchen floor, I remembered what the neighbour had said about people with names like Kulyk.

RUTH   Karen lived in a big beautiful house with two staircases covered in thick, plush royal blue carpets and floor-to-ceiling windows swathed in velvet drapes. She knew about kissing boys and I was smitten. She was so cool. One day we were playing in her beautiful bedroom on the four-poster canopy bed when her mother said it was time for me to go home. "Why?" she asked.

"Because we are going to the club," her mother replied.

"Can't she come with us?" she asked.

"No," her mother replied.

"Why?" she asked.

"Because she's Jewish."

POLLY   When I was eight, Jankey Persad-Moon had a crush on me, but he was a *chamar*, or what was referred to in those days as an untouchable, so I never spoke to him. When I discovered that his mother was a *chamine*, the midwife who had attended to my sister, I had to tell him. He was so thrilled that he rolled up his exercise book, put it to my ear, and began to sing the latest Hindi love song... (FRANCINE *holds a paper tube to* POLLY's *ear.*)

"Jee ah beeka rar hai Chayee behar hai Aja mera balma..."

The class had become unusually quiet. All eyes were on us.

JUDITH THOMPSON

GLENDA   I was maybe six and all the kookums were having their morning bath in the lake. They all had their long slips on. I was watching them. It wasn't my turn but I jumped in anyway. I decided to sneak in under water and there I saw *my* kookum's grey slip. So I took a great big gulp of water in my mouth and then I emerged and with a fountain full of water, I spouted it from my mouth. My kookum chuckled and said, "Oh you!"

JUDY   It's my ninth birthday. I invited all my friends but especially Billy Wellwood. I had a crush on him. When it came time to open my presents, he sheepishly hands me this box. I am really hoping it's a necklace or a bracelet. I unwrapped the box and there, under the tissue paper, were three pairs of white underpants.

ANN MARIE   My grandfather Alfonse, this man was six feet, nine inches tall, and he smelled like a garden. He grew yams, cassava, and okra and sold them at the market. No one could rob him one penny, but my grandfather couldn't read or write. Here I was, his eight-year-old granddaughter teaching my grandfather to read. See Spot run… Walk Jane walk.

BARBIE   At my elementary school we were divided into four what they called "houses." Wrens, Robins, Swallows, and Hummingbirds. I was a Hummingbird. Every Monday morning, the girls who had done something wrong were made to stand up at the assembly cloaked in shame as our atrocities were described. Things like taking your scissors to the library or not wearing your gloves on the bus. Running in the hall. Really *bad* things. So there I was every Monday. Every Monday. I remember a teacher once said to me, "You are the worst Hummingbird in the history of this school." Ask me? I am the worst Hummingbird in the history of space and time. I just want you to know who you're dealing with.

LOIS   I was about six years old, with a beautiful low voice. Very low. Too low, apparently, for a girl. My parents took me to the Montreal Children's Hospital—Voice Pathology—the doctor was pretty sure they could fix it without an operation if I did these voice exercises every day, and she showed me how to take my earlobes and turn them inside out, raise up my neck, and in the highest voice repeat after her: "Sweet meat, neat seat, eat feet, sweet meat." I was diligent, practising every day, just like she showed me. When

10

the kids on my street rang my bell to see if I could come out and play, my parents said I was busy. I thought they went away, but they must have spied on me, because when I came out to play, everyone had their hands on their earlobes, and everyone's earlobes were turned inside out and everyone was saying:

ALL   (*holding their earlobes*) "Sweet meat, neat seat, eat feet, sweet meat..."

PAULINE   Every day when I went to school, my aunt put my hair in two big ugly plaits. I hated it. So I go to my friend Eileen's house, she still had the fire going from breakfast. We took the plait out. We put the fork in the fire to heat it up. I had to hold the fork with a cloth so I wouldn't get burnt. I would straighten my hair piece by piece, so it would look nice and silky to impress the boys. It works better than going to the hairdresser. It looks beautiful, but please don't try this at home. I'm a hairdresser, I know it.

JOANNA   We left our reserve in Saskatchewan to move to BC when I was five years old. Soon after we became very, very poor. I became very resourceful as a young child. I collected wires to strip for copper, I went bottle hunting for cash, I delivered papers, and knocked on doors to do chores. And then I discovered the church. I discovered that if I attended their Bible classes they would feed me. Kool-Aid, cookies, cakes, sandwiches, real milk. I learned Genesis, Exodus, Leviticus, all of it. They thought I was the perfect little red Indian girl. But I also learned that good girls went to heaven and bad girls went to hell. Then one day I realized that because I was only going to church for the food, I was going straight to hell.

FRANCINE   My dad, Fred, worked late many nights a week, and on Saturdays too. Sunday was family day. What he liked best was lying on the couch and he'd give us a comb and get my sister and myself to comb his hair and search for lice. Now, no need to tell you, we never found lice. We would comb his hair for what seemed like hours. Hours. And every once in while he would sigh. And when we heard the sigh we knew he was happy.

GLORIA   1957. Brooklyn was becoming riddled with gangs. My mother's fear caused her to send my sister and myself south to live with an aunt and uncle who had no children. She put us on a bus heading to North Carolina. Five hours out of New York, the bus came to a rest stop. My sister and I got off and went into the restaurant and sat down. Three times the waitress passed us by. Finally, I called, "Miss? Miss?" Turning around she snarled, "You kids get out of here!" My older sister was quiet but even then I had a mouth. I said, "We have money, we can pay." Just as I stood, walking towards us was this big man with this huge protruding stomach. I remember how his belly looked like a ball with a belt circling underneath it. As he approached us I think he realized that we really didn't know the rules. "Now listen here, you chil'ens, you here in the South now, this he-ah's the Mason-Dixon line. You can't come in here. You see that sign out tha... (RUTH *raises a sign above her head that reads* "COLORED.") ...you want something to eat you go to that window, git your food, and git back on the bus." We got back on that bus, but my sister and I, we never ate, drank, or went to the bathroom until we reached Landis, North Carolina.

RHONDA   I met my father for the first time when I was turning twelve. My parents had been separated for eleven years. My father was the only member of his family to survive Auschwitz. He remained broken and damaged for the rest of his life. My mother took us to the Bathurst and Bloor subway station. He waited for us in the space between bus and streetcar. He took us to a greasy restaurant with green leather booths. We ate hamburgers. He bent over, smiled at us, and wanted to know, "When will you call me 'Dad'?"

CAROLYN   When I was nine years old I saw myself sleeping in my bed. I was watching from the ceiling. I thought, "I'd better get down there before she wakes up or she'll be dead." When I woke up I knew this was something extraordinary. When I told Edie, my adored nanny, about this, she said, "Oh darling, that was just a dream." I never spoke of it to anybody else, but I knew it was real. As a little girl I felt I had been given a rare and unfathomable gift. I still do. It is as clear today as it was seventy years ago.

JEANNINE   September. First day in school. The teachers were meaning business. At six years old, my first day in school, I learned to write "A" in cursive, but what I only saw on the blackboard were these (*makes the shape of a single vertical line with her finger*) and I produced a full page of (*makes the shape of a single vertical line again*) and very proud I showed the teacher and she said, "*Petite dinde.* Are you a stupid little turkey?" I was badly needing glasses.

Teenagers

A lively piece of dance music that was popular twenty to thirty years ago blasts as the women put on "teenager" clothes and dance around the stage. The music stops for each woman's story while the rest of the group pauses mid-dance.

JANICE   When I was sixteen my parents sent me off for the summer to Winnipeg, to study Ukrainian at a college there, a cross between ethnic summer camp and reform school. At first I was so miserable that I stopped eating; when I came home my sister didn't recognize me. But I did I fall in love with a boy whose last name was Vovk, which means Wolf, and he was one hundred percent lamb. I was so innocent that I thought necking meant sticking out your chin; I was tortured by the thought that the first time he kissed me our noses would crash together. It never occurred to me that you could simply tilt your head and keep breathing. The rest of my captivity flew by, thanks to my lamb in wolf's clothing, who returned to Minnesota, got sent to Vietnam, and still wanders through my dreams from time to time, a sweet, black-haired boy, leading with his chin.

RUTH   I spent my adolescence in a socialist youth group. Girls and boys were all equal. Except we weren't and I didn't figure it out until I was eighteen, a head counsellor at the summer camp. The boys, my friends, challenged me at every turn. The night before camp started I ran a meeting to run through rules for my staff. I kept getting interrupted by a counsellor and I responded with, "Wait your turn." When I was done I turned to him and said, "What was it you so badly needed to say?" And he said, "Hey everybody, if you get a chance—fuck Ruth."

POLLY   When I was fifteen years old Boysie kissed me in the rain and I melted. That night I prayed and prayed and prayed that I wouldn't get pregnant.

GLENDA By the time I was sixteen, I was in survival mode. I thought I needed a man to take care of me, so I shacked up with Hughie. We were at a party. He punched me, he kicked me, and he choked me and he said he was going to kill me. And then we went home together, I thought I was in love.

ANN MARIE The first time I smoked ganja I tried to cross the street and all I could see was the yellow line moving back and forth, wavy. It was the first and last time with ganja.

BARBIE I can tell you when I became a rock-hard feminist. When I was in university, I got a call early one morning from a boy I knew at a fraternity. He asked if I could come over because there was a young girl who was roaming the halls wrapped in only a sheet. She was only sixteen and, until that night, a virgin. There had been a lineup all night outside the bedroom she stayed in. But now it was morning and what were they supposed to do with her? Call Barbie, I guess. I drove her to Women's College for a morning-after pill, which I'm sure made her *really* sick, and then took her home. And in the car she kept saying, "You're so lucky to be friends with such a great bunch of guys."

LOIS I was sixteen—growing up in the suburbs of Montreal. I was a secret little baby butch, surrounded by a flock of boy-crazy teenage girls. On the outside I was popular, the phone rang off the hook. But inside, I was alone. Searingly, achingly alone. I don't even remember thinking much about it—I reached for the cupboard and counted out twenty-two 222s onto the kitchen counter—I put them in a pattern of stars and I took them, a pill and a sip of water, a pill and a sip of water, a pill and a sip of water, until I had taken all twenty-two and then I went off to school. They sent me home and I went to bed with my boots still on. At the hospital, the doctors said it was encephalitis. For twenty-five years I never told a soul.

PAULINE My aunt would force me to carry water to this old man's house and every time I take the water to him, he touch me on my boobs, he touch me on my bum. I told my aunt every time I carry water for him he touch me on my boob, he touch me on my bum. But she did not believe me and forced me to go back. So when I carry water for him, I leave it at the door and he has to *crawl* and get it.

FRANCINE   Fatigué after a long day skiing, we got into the overheated and dark bus. As I sat down, André, l'instructeur de ski, à la peau basanée et aux yeux d'un tigre noir, nested right beside me. Well the bus had hardly left when he started to kiss me passionately. After a while I felt my bottom lip being sucked away from my face; I quite liked it. Then he was gone. Well as we arrived at the bus terminal, anxious to tell my friends all about it, I started walking towards them to find out they too all had a swollen lip.

JOANNA   When I was a young teenager every summer weekend was spent dancing with my father and elders at powwows all over the North American plains. They wouldn't let me near anyone under the age of sixty. I was *so* bored. Until one day at the Thunderchild powwow I saw a gorgeous Oklahoma grass dancer. I fell madly in love. He delivered flour, sugar, tea, lard, and deer meat to our camp. I thought for sure they would invite him in to join us but they never did. So we would do the dance of the eyes, the dance where your eyes meet and there's a knowing and a stirring in your body, where your hearts are never broken. My Oklahoma grass dancer would come and torment my father by dancing in front of me. His eyes would lock on mine. (JOANNA *begins her dance while* RUTH *rattles.* JOANNA *dances low to the ground and does the whoop.*) Whoooo! Whooo! Whoooo-ooo!

RHONDA   It was a cold and snowy December evening when I entered the restaurant. I said, "Hello," and smiled. He gestured that we go in and sit at one of the tables. He could not speak. He started using sign language. Not yet twenty, I did not know any sign language. In a terrifying high-pitched voice, he told me that as a deaf woman, the odds of me finding a compatible man were very low and therefore I should choose him. When I got home that evening thirty years ago, I vomited and sobbed and turned to my mother and asked her: "What am I supposed to become?"

CAROLYN   I was fourteen, riding home on the London tube one evening with my twenty-year-old cousin, April. There were only a couple of other people in our car, and one was sitting opposite us. He was a nondescript, middle-aged man wearing a raincoat. He suddenly opened the coat and exposed his flaccid and rather purple penis. I had never seen or imagined anything like this so I went into a state of sheer panic—April immediately pulled me up and steered me to the other end of the car, saying in a rather loud voice, "That's a very little thing to be worried about, Carolyn!"

JEANNINE   On my seventeenth birthday, I went to a convent to become a nun. We had to take vows of poverty, obedience, and chastity. I didn't know the meaning of the word chastity. So I asked the padre, "What am I sacrificing by the vow of chastity?" He told me, "Girl, what you don't know won't hurt you."

The music continues as the women put away their teenager costumes and go to the structures.

Mothers' Stories

As each woman tells her story she approaches upstage middle.

JANICE   My beautiful, talented, powerful mother. Who stayed up all night sewing exquisite dresses for me, and who told me over and over that she should have strangled me in my cradle. Who praised me to the sky to others, but to my face called me ugly, clumsy, and stupid, teaching me to hate myself. Only after she died could I walk into her house without fear thundering in my heart.

RUTH   When I was diagnosed with cancer, my mother came with me to every appointment, held my hand, chauffeured me, did laundry, prepared meals, tucked me in at night—just like a mother. I was twenty years too young for my cancer diagnosis. But there it was. When the doctor walked into the room at an appointment, he looked at my mother and said, "Ms. Rakoff." My mother replied, "It should be me."

POLLY   My mother died at the age that I am now. She had been placed in an arranged marriage at age thirteen; had her first child at eighteen and, still blessed by the goddess Lakshmi, her twelfth at fifty. She died on the eve of my twenty-fifth birthday and for ten years after I did not celebrate my birthday.

GLENDA   My mother was forced to go to residential school. One day she was punished for speaking her language, Cree. The nun pulled her up three flights of stairs by her braid. She gave her a tooth-brush and told her to brush the stairs all the way down and to "do a good job." My mother was a storyteller and had a wonderful sense of humour. Despite the brutal legacy of the residential schools, our home was always filled with love and laughter. This was the mother I hung onto when she gave in to her pain.

JUDY   My mother grew up in Brockville where her parents ran the only Chinese restaurant. Her father almost gambled the restaurant away. After he shot himself, my grandma, my popo, carried on, worked off his debts and turned the restaurant into a great success. When my mother left my father, my powerful father, after living for thirty-two years in his shadow, I understood that my popo had passed on to my mum her gutsiness.

ANN MARIE   I was three months old when my grandmother took me in. By the time I was fifteen I longed to know what a mother's love was like. I went back to my mother's house. There were seven other kids and too many chores to do. It was too crowded. I didn't find what I was looking for. I ran to my grandmother's house, where I belonged.

BARBIE   My mother, Lizzie, had a very quick, dark sense of humour. One night she was asleep in bed up at our summer cottage near Powell River and my friend Willy MacIntyre got her bedroom window mixed up with my bedroom window. (LOIS *jumps beside* BARBIE *and throws her arms around her.*) Suddenly my mother found her-self… in an embrace, and from a sound sleep, without missing a beat, sat up and said, "Well, *hello* Willy."

LOIS   It would be December and my mom would say, "It's cold outside," and my dad would say, "Just like a cold day in December." She would crack up. At night, in bed, Ed McMahon would come on and my father would go, "Here's Johnny!" That would get her every time. I went to sleep every night with the sound of my mother laughing. When he died, they were both fifty-four years old. I met her in the hospital—she was standing in the doorway of his room waiting for me. I came towards her and she just grabbed me and said, "I LOVE YOU I LOVE YOU I LOVE YOU I LOVE YOU I LOVE YOU…"

PAULINE   The first time I met my mother I was fourteen years old. I went to her house and she told me not to call her "Mummy." I had to call

17

her Aunt Urith. She didn't want her friends to know she had us. Thirty-five years later my mother called, two o'clock in the morning, and apologized for leaving us. She said when she divorced our father, she divorced us also. Christmas gone, she phoned me and for the first time in my life told me she loves me.

JOANNA   As my mother lay dying at age sixty, I caressed and kissed her feet and hands. I marvelled at all the love and hard work those hands had given. The thousands of miles those feet had walked. I took the eagle feather, sweet grass, and sage that I had hung on her hospital bed and went outside and for the first time prayed with anger in my voice. I prayed for my ancestors to come and relieve her of her suffering. Later that evening as my sister and I were in her hospital room, the room had become very full. Our ancestors had come to take her home.

CAROLYN   When I was nineteen, I came home one night to my mother's apartment in London and noticed ashes in the living-room fireplace, which was odd, because she never used the fireplace. There was a note on her bedroom door saying, "Very tired, please don't disturb." I slept on the sofa when I stayed with her; luckily, because I was awakened in the morning by very loud snoring coming from my mother's room... I tried to wake her up, but she was unconscious. I rang the family doctor who called an ambulance. She had taken enough Phenobarbital, as the doctor said, to kill a horse. At the hospital, her stomach was pumped and she remained in a deep sleep for days. When finally conscious, she cursed loudly at everyone in sight. When she came home she said to me, "Why did you call the doctor?" I said, "I didn't want you to die, I love you." She said, "How dare you interfere with my life." Those ashes in the fireplace were forty-year-old love letters from her fiancé who died in a plane crash three months before they were to be married.

GLORIA   My mother lived her life by her sayings, some of which governed men, especially since she was married four times. She was widowed once, divorced twice, and married for the fourth and final time at the age of fifty. "Men are like trains," she would say. "Every five minutes there's another one coming along." "A man without a moustache is like eating an egg without salt." "Start out the way you want to end up." This covered everything from married life to self-image. I believe my mother was a true feminist without knowing it, except when she said, "A whistling woman and a crowing hen always come to no good end."

RHONDA   My mother grew up in a house near Kensington Market where she slept in the attic. She had to leave high school at the age of fourteen because back then accommodations were not made for deaf students. She went to work in her uncle's coat factory on Spadina, where she sewed buttons and checked inseams. To this day, I never visit Kensington Market without pausing in front of the red-brick house on Oxford Street.

JEANNINE   My mother was a schizophrenic. She was never happy. I would dream that one day she would look at me, see me, and love me. Just after she had died of Alzheimer's at eighty-one years old, I looked at her and I thought she was finally at peace. She seemed to be smiling at me, for the first time in my life.

FRANCINE   Maman. (*heavy sigh*). Oh! ma mère…

At the first sound of a thunderstorm, she would order my sister and me to follow her into the dark darkness of the wardrobe where she would splash holy water at us until the storm ended. Ô mon Dieu!

Compliments # 1

Each pair comes together in the middle of the structure, then walks the catwalk to downstage centre to deliver their compliment. The violin accompanies.

JANICE   I walk like the wind.
RUTH   I have spectacular tits.

GLENDA   I have a beautiful back.
LOIS   I have killer bedroom eyes.

CAROLYN   I have strong and shapely shoulders.
JUDY   I have luscious lips.

GLORIA   I have a devastating smile

BARBIE   This is so embarrassing to say this kind of thing about yourself, but I have *excellent* posture.

POLLY   I have the neck of a swan.

PAULINE   I have a hot booty.

FRANCINE   J'ai des jambes tentatrices.

RHONDA   I have ravishing curls.

ANN MARIE   I'm tall and elegant.

JOANNA   I stand strong on the land.

CAROLYN & JEANNINE
     Who in the audience can do this at seventy-nine /eighty?

CAROLYN and JEANNINE touch the floor.

Insults

The women stand and sit around the structure.

JANICE   "Ugly cow!"

RUTH   "You got the biggest goddamn ass."

POLLY   "Curry mouth."

ANN MARIE   "Witchiepoo."

BARBIE   "You used to be quite good looking."

JOANNA   "Hey cutie, where's your booty?"

LOIS   "Ewwww, ugly nipples."

PAULINE   "Lord, ya fat-ee!"

GLENDA	"You with your double chin."
JUDY	"Flat as a skateboard."
FRANCINE	"Hey, l'échalote. Ton père travailles-tu pour la compagnie d'toothpick?"
GLORIA	"Flat butt."
RHONDA	"You better lose that ass if you ever want to meet a guy."
JEANNINE	Comme j'étais très maigre mon père me disait, "Tu es comme un hareng venu du Manitoba à pied." My father said, because I was so lean, "You look like a herring that walked from Manitoba on foot."
CAROLYN	"What with your unfashionably large mouth and ice-cold feet you'll never find a husband!"

Compliments # 2

The women repeat the same catwalk from the previous "Compliments" while the violin accompanies.

JANICE	She has a waist like water.
ANN MARIE	And she is so slinky.
BARBIE	Ruthie *does* have *spectacular*... olive skin tone.
RUTH	Her nails are nothing a manicure wouldn't fix.
POLLY	She has a voice like caramel.
LOIS	Her hands speak a language all their own.
FRANCINE	Regardez ces mignons petits petons.
RHONDA	Check out that striking head of hair.
GLENDA	Her eyes shine like the moon.
PAULINE	When I look at her I see the sun coming out.

| BARBIE | She is as lithe as a willow wand. |
| JUDY | Every part of her is alive. |

CAROLYN & JEANNINE
If I were her, I wouldn't change a thing.

| GLORIA | And she has a beautiful face, doesn't she. |

Leaving Home

The women form a chain with their arms. During their stories FRANCINE, GLORIA, JOANNA, BARBIE, *and* CAROLYN *peak or break through the chain.*

| FRANCINE | I was twenty-one when I finally told my mother I was leaving. She was so upset that she ran upstairs, crying, yelling, "You don't love me! You don't love me!" I ran after her and sat her down and told her, "I love you, I do love you. That's why I have to go!" |

| GLORIA | I never wanted to leave my mother's house. My greatest comfort was found under her roof. I hope my children find that same comfort under my roof. |

| BARBIE | Bad Hummingbird that I was, it was off to boarding school for me. The catch was—I wasn't allowed to come home. I had a headache that lasted months. It was the first time I ever thought about suicide. I became anorexic. I decided I would develop a protective persona: funny, cavalier, cutting, wild, slutty, tough. My party trick in college was to throw myself down a flight of stairs. |

| CAROLYN | I couldn't wait to leave my unhappy mother. I sat in the train, excited, scared, thrilled, nervous, and feeling as free as a bird. |

| JEANNINE | Leaving home for me was like un papillon qui s'envole. |

Under music, GLENDA *climbs the structure and picks up a drum.*

| GLENDA | Home left me when I was thirteen. I pressed my face and hands against the small window that had crystallized from the minus |

thirty-degree weather outside. My gaze was fixed on my mom as she placed suitcases in the trunk of the taxi. I so desperately hoped my mother would come back in or tell us to grab our jackets quickly, that the meter in the taxi was costing her, or that this was some kind a joke. The taxi turned off its light and drove off. I walked away from the window and away from my youth. My sister and I were alone. I stood there for a few moments and then I said to my sister, "Let's go." All I could hear was the snow crunch, and we made our way to find a phone. Many years later my mom invited me over and when I walked into her house I knew what she was going to say. Her hand was shaking and her head was shaking and she said, "My girl, I am sorry, I am truly, truly sorry."

Women's Warrior Song

GLENDA *drums and sings a Cree women's warrior song while standing high on the structure, stage right. The women gather around her.*

Four drum beats.

ALL   Ya – E – Oh – Oh, Ya – E – Oh – Oh
Hey, Hey Ya – E – Oh – Oh
Ya – E – Oh –
Hey, Hey Ya – E – Oh

Two drum beats.

Hey, Hey, Hey
Ya – E – Oh – Oh, Ya – E – Oh – Oh
Hey, Hey Ya – E – Oh
Ya – E – Oh – Oh
Hey, Hey Ya – E – Oh

Two drum beats.

She raises her hand and sings without the drum.

23

A Woman

The women stay gathered around the structure stage right. As they each tell their story they find their place within two horizontal lines downstage, with the violin covering their walk.

JANICE   My mother came to stay with us when I was about to give birth to my second child. The night before I gave birth we were in the kitchen, sitting at the table with the scarred enamel top, my keepsake from the grandmother whose love for me was the foundation of my life. "Janice," she said, "you should have heard what your nana would say about you. You think she really loved *you?*" I staggered and then somehow I found the strength to fight back: "I know she did!" That was the moment I stopped being a cowed, beaten little girl and I became a woman.

RUTH   On my sixth-grade report card the comments from all my teachers read, "Ruth argues too much." And I did. I questioned everything. Over the years, much effort was put into trying to shut me up. At eighteen, when I was about to be thrown out of school overseas for… energetic questioning, I was given a choice. They said I could agree to be a good girl or I could leave the program. And it occurred to me, at that moment, that if being a good girl meant blindly accepting untruths, illusions, and propaganda, then I would never be a good girl. I would be a woman who always questions everything.

POLLY   I knew I was a woman when I got my daughter back. Because of a difficult divorce when my daughter was three, I had to kidnap her from her father's house. She was playing in the garden. It had been a long time since I had seen her and she did not know me. My mother-in-law opened up the gate and I went down and I grabbed her and said, "Here, sweetheart, come with me!" We took nothing. No toys, no clothes, no shoes, nothing. We drove away and she was screaming: "I want my Aunty Sandra," but I was holding in my arms what was most precious to me in the world.

ANN MARIE   I left home at the age of nineteen to live with a man of my dreams; my Rasta man took me away to live in the country. We cooked okra, we drank coconut water. Sometimes we had no food. For a time, it was worth it to live for love, but when I had my baby, I changed. I needed to feed my baby, so I took my baby back home to my grandmother's house. Now I was a woman.

BARBIE   I've never related to the milestones that they say make you a woman. I didn't want to have children. I didn't want to get married. When I was little, I felt like a very *old* child. Now? I feel like a very *old* child.

LOIS   I first thought being grown up meant I could get as drunk and stoned as I wanted. So I did. One day I fell on my lover and she said, "Look, you want to be a falling-down drunk, go ahead, but you will not pull me down with you."

JOANNA   I was seventeen when I had my first child. I didn't know what to do. I was confused, frightened. I didn't know what to do; everyone around me was saying give her up. Everyone except for this lovely off-the-wall social worker who told me, "You can keep your baby." I thought long and hard, and then a few days later I picked up the phone and asked Mary for help. She came and picked me up, we drove to Mississauga to the temporary foster home. They opened the door and handed me Jennifer, the most beautiful baby girl in the world. She looked right into my eyes and gurgled when I kissed her cheek. When I held her, I knew that the universe was unfolding as it should, my ancestors were smiling. We began our life together. Girl, woman, and child.

PAULINE   I felt grown up when I bought my first can of condensed milk with my own money. When I was little, I would always sip the condensed milk from the can and I would get beaten. So the first time I bought my own can of condensed milk I drank the whole can.

GLENDA   As you know I was forced to grow up at thirteen. I was forced to become a woman before my time.

JUDY   Two years after my husband died, I went online to find another man. I thought I needed to be married to be happy. That was a lie. Being in this play with these women telling only true stories gave me the guts to say to my second husband, "I am in this for the wrong reasons." Thank you, Mum, thank you, Popo.

JUDITH THOMPSON

GLORIA   I reached adulthood locked in a filthy chain-gang jail in 1963.
          The route from Brooklyn to Landis led me finally to Greensboro,
          North Carolina. Here, amid voices that cried "Jail over bail" and
          "We shall overcome." I found my life's path.

RHONDA   I couldn't hear. It was 1977. I was beginning my undergradu-
          ate degree. I was excited and passionate about literature. But the
          classes were too big. If I didn't cross campus on time I didn't get
          a front seat. So I sat in front of the Royal Ontario Museum and
          I cried. The next day was a Friday and I went to see the dean. I
          explained. I was committed to doing the work, but I had to have
          a front seat. She said consider it done. Monday morning I had
          front seats reserved. That's when I learned that even though I
          couldn't hear, I could be heard.

CAROLYN   I married a kind and brilliant man who at times became a violent
          and delusional maniac when drinking; which was almost every
          night. I finally left him early one morning with three children un-
          der five, an elderly family member who had lived with us since I
          was two years old, and two cats. I had twenty dollars in my wallet,
          the clothes we were wearing, and nothing else. I drove to Toronto,
          three hours away, I found a job and a place for us to live without
          sadness or fear, and I became a woman.

JEANNINE I was a late, late bloomer. I had the feeling that I was walking be-
          side my life most of the time. I decided that it was better for me
          just to have friends. But then it happened. I was forty-three when
          love fell on me.

FRANCINE 1950. It all took place into that dark, smelly, musty basement.
          After a while, he let me go and said SHHHHH. He was the next-
          door neighbour. As I grew up a part of me stayed in that base-
          ment. After many years I found the courage to climb those stairs
          and there it was, womanhood, in all its beauty. As unexpected
          and breathtaking as a falling star.

          *The women perform a slow, unified movement to an appropri-
          ate piece of music. They raise their hands to the ceiling and bring
          their arms down, right then left, watching their hands. From
          stage right they make their way across the stage, exiting stage left.*

RUTH *dances with* PAULINE *before leaving.* PAULINE *dances off-stage as the lights fade.*

End of Act One.

Act Two

Crones

All enter to low, ominous music from stage left and form a tight circle, crouching together as a coven. Their low cackles build in volume until they burst out of their formation.

JANICE	BABA YAGA
RUTH	MACH SHEFA
POLLY	SOUCOUYANT
ANN MARIE	MAMA DLO
BARBIE	OLD BAT
LOIS	LA STREGA
PAULINE	DUPPY
JOANNA	ASKEESH

GLENDA	MUCHIE MANITOU
JUDY	NYU WUU
FRANCINE	DIABLESSE
GLORIA	BANSHEE
CAROLYN	VIRAGO

> RHONDA *walks through the coven to downstage centre. With* RHONDA *taking the lead, all the women undo their cloaks and drop them to the floor, revealing their stunning gowns.*

RHONDA   (*signs only*) ANGEL

ALL   (*signs only*) ANGEL

RHONDA   ANGEL

> *The women pick up their cloaks as an instrumental of "Lust" begins on violin. Under the music,* LOIS *gets her guitar, sits on the centre of the structure, and begins her song. Women slowly exit with cloaks.*

Lois Sings Lust

> As LOIS *sings, the women exit with cloaks and then joyfully join* LOIS *on the structure, placing themselves for erotic stories. Some lounge, some sit on and around the structure, which is now raised to form a long table.*

LOIS   In a downtown café, in a downtown frame of mind
We let go our clichés as a sign of the times
We drank beer though it was early, and the jazz music played
We laughed hard, people looked, at the jokes that you made
There were flowers on the table that the boys had sent to us
And we would have even thanked them but we couldn't
We were in lust, we were in lust.

My hand reaches under the table, your face gives nothing away
I smile at our secret but really I just can't wait
To get home—home—home—home

Well we went to my apartment; we got in with your key
Then we raced for the bathroom, cuz we both had to pee
Then I read you some poems, you read between the lines
Our bodies anticipating what we had on our minds
Now there's something to be said about sincerity and trust
But those things they don't compare, they don't compare to our lust
To our lust

Erotic

*The women lounge around the structure as they listen to each
other's erotic story.*

JANICE   When I was nineteen, my mother decided I was ready for fur—
and so we went to a wholesaler to order a fox-fur coat, the colour of
buckwheat honey. The idea was that I would wear it every Sunday
all the next winter to St. Demetrius Ukrainian Greek Orthodox
Church, that seething hotbed of eligible Ukrainian bachelors.
The coat took much longer to make up than expected and before
it was ready I fell headlong into love and marriage. My mother
didn't approve of my husband; he was long-haired and bearded
and definitely not Ukrainian. She insisted that the furrier sew my
maiden name into the lining of the coat, in a heavy satin stitch.
The coat finally arrived one summer afternoon while my husband
was at work; I waited for him hour after hot and humid hour, in
our cockroach-infested flat with the peeling paint and sagging sun
porch. And when I heard him unlock the front door, I sprang into
his arms, wearing my fox-fur coat and nothing else.

RUTH   It was August in Quebec City with my husband; we had dumped
our kids with my in-laws and off we went; we saw a cool dress in
the store window. He said, "Go on in and try it on." "No, it's too
short." But he insisted, so I put on the dress and I shouted out from
the dressing room, "It's too tight." And he said, "Come out." And I
walked out of the dressing room and the salesgirl said, "Oooh lala."

31

And then a couple walked into the store and they said, "Wow!" So I bought two of them. We went back to the B&B that night and I went to take a bath. I thought we were the only people staying there and I hadn't taken anything with me to change into except this dress. And as I was soaking in the bath I heard other people walking up the stairs and I didn't have a towel. I got out of the bath, and threw the dress on my wet steaming body and went into the room. My husband looked at me in the dress and it didn't stay on for long.

CAROLYN My first acting job after theatre school, and in gorgeous Penzance, Cornwall, where the leading man was also gorgeous. I could sense his attraction to me, but I was eighteen and a virgin, and he was in his late twenties and fortunately for me (or unfortunately), a true gentleman. Our cast would travel in a large van to perform in towns outside of Penzance and he always sat next to me and put his arm around me. No more than that. Sometimes I would lay my head on his shoulder and try to sleep. His name was John and I will never forget him, or that delicious electricity.

POLLY I was in Nepal on a teaching contract. He was a building engineer. I met him through my colleagues. He offered Chinese cigarettes to them proclaiming them to be the best in the world. After his persistence I finally agreed to have dinner with him. We drank his favourite plum wine. He ordered an array of tantalizing live shrimp that we cooked in the hotpot. When his black velvet eyes looked deeply into mine I knew I would not resist a kiss. As we walked back home, he asked me to his room, and although he was enticing I said, "Don't hold your breath." After all I was forty-nine and he was twenty-nine. For the next few days, we didn't see much of each other. But there was still this burning wish. As I was leaving, the front desk gave me a gift box and a note; the gift was a delicate, carved, sandalwood-scented fan. The note said "I am still holding my breath."

ANN MARIE I'll tell you the truth, I'm still holding my breath too.

JUDY It was the middle of the night and I couldn't sleep. My husband was snoring but I didn't mind because if he was snoring it meant he was still alive. I remember running my fingers through hair, stroking his eyelids. I would lean into his sleeping body and brush my lips against his. I was memorizing him.

BARBIE   Here's something I think about sex: I hate it when people seem to have some kind of lovemaking technique. When you feel they're enacting something they've read about in some manual or book. You can almost hear the pages flipping. As far as I'm concerned if you have that sort of appetite for someone, all they really have to do is show up. Good in bed? Bad in bed? It's *who's* in bed.

FRANCINE   It's true, Barbie. I had never felt anything like this before. It came out of nowhere. We were in bed and I found myself touching his hand. I was suddenly charged with the sole desire to caress, feel his palm, his mound of Venus, his fingers, his lengthy fingers, twisting and twirling them. This contortion led to a *pas de quatre* that crescendoed into flapping and pinching. It lasted nearly two hours. C'était la première et la dernière fois.

GLORIA   Once my husband and I participated in a contest with four other couples. The eyes of the five wives were blindfolded, and using our noses we had to smell the legs of all five men, choosing our mate. If you can believe that lust is having the scent in your nose of the person you want—I found my man!

RHONDA   Once I took a trip to Italy with my in-laws. My husband at the time had to be somewhere else. I was still a newlywed. We took the train to Florence and then spent a few days driving through Tuscany. We stopped for lunch one day in a little hamlet. It was late and the place was empty. A woman offered to fix us lunch from whatever was left in the kitchen. We were the only ones there. Then, a group of dusty, well-tanned construction workers came in. Lunch was over; I headed to the bathroom before we got back into the car. Walking through the café, I took a little glance at one of them. He looked at me too. There was electricity. It was powerful. I finished my business in the bathroom cubicle and came out to wash my hands and there he was. His body curved, staring at me from the doorframe, his arms were all the warm, sun-baked hills of Tuscany; and all the olive oil in Italy was in his eyes. So I smiled and said, "Hi!" And I washed my hands and then moved towards him to leave the bathroom. And I said, "I have to go now." And just before he moved aside to let me pass, he whispered with a half-smile, "Ciao."

Having Children

RUTH   So sometimes all this heat and electricity leads to pregnancy.

When I got pregnant for the first time, I read through all the pregnancy books. One book in particular suggested that instead of rushing to the hospital at the first signs of labour, I should take my time and perhaps prepare some sandwiches for my labour coach. I took the book and threw it against the wall. Let him prepare his own fucking sandwiches! I'm a little busy having a baby! If my husband complains about a minor ache or pain or perhaps even something as serious as a man cold, I reply... *(lifts legs up high and yells as if she is giving birth)*

JANICE   I have two beautiful sons, six-foot-four and six-foot-nine. And sometimes I wish they were still small enough to cradle in my arms.

RUTH   Three ugly, ugly boys. She lo niphtach peh la satan. And they question everything.

POLLY   One daughter named Karma. A powerful self-reliant artist who is living in Berlin; as far away from me as she could get.

ANN MARIE   Three children, twenty-six, nineteen, fifteen, all their own person. And they are driving me crazy.

BARBIE   I have—let me think—two sets of ex-common-law step-grandchildren. One side calls me Bubbie, the other side calls me Grannie Barb.

LOIS   I have a twenty-four-year-old son and a seventeen-year-old daughter, and even though none of us share a speck of DNA, they both look exactly like me.

PAULINE   Me have two sons who don't give me no trouble, and three daughters who work hard like me but very jealous of each other. And between all of them, they have eleven children.

GLENDA   We have six children, his and mine, and ten beautiful grandbabies.

JUDY   Three teenagers. Raising them without their dad has been the hardest thing I've ever done, but it is also (*beat*) unendingly rich.

JOANNA   I have three heroes I call my daughters. I learn so much from them.

FRANCINE   Trois enfants très indépendants, je dirais même trop indépendants, deux petits anges, un petit fils, une petite fille.

RHONDA   I have two formidable teenage daughters.

CAROLYN   I have three children in their fifties and four grandchildren. Our blended family consists of seven children and thirteen grandchildren. How lucky is this only child.

GLORIA   Me? I have two daughters, a rocket scientist and an idiot. The roles change daily.

JEANNINE   Even though I decided never to have children because of la violence dans ma famille et ma solitude, during ménopause I mourned the children I never had.

FRANCINE   C'est incroyable, Jeannine.

JEANNINE   Don't worry, Francine. Not anymore.

Accomplishments

The violin plays as the women form a line and introduce each other, to comical, simple, Gilbert-and-Sullivan flavoured music, recorded piano.

ALL   Welcome to our dinner party!

BARBIE   Let us introduce you to our guests.

BARBIE / RHONDA

Rhonda learned to sign at age twenty-four and she is a teacher of the deaf.

RHONDA / POLLY

> Polly was principal of Heritage Education with a staff of seventy-five teaching forty-five languages.

POLLY / PAULINE

> Pauline has a doctorate in cosmetology and two successful professional salons.

PAULINE / GLENDA

> Glenda is a front-line community support worker for women fleeing abuse.

GLENDA / LOIS

> Lois is a CGA and Director of Finance of a project worth $78 million.

LOIS / CAROLYN

> Carolyn is an award-winning actor in theatre, film, and television.

CAROLYN / GLORIA

> Gloria was a therapist for the elderly.

GLORIA / ANN MARIE

> Ann Marie works with autistic children and she has the bite marks to prove it.

ANN MARIE / JANICE

> Janice has published fourteen books and won six major literary awards.

JANICE / JUDY

> Judy, who writes for a hospice, overcame her pain and grief and helps other young widows.

JUDY / FRANCINE

> Francine helps the self-esteem of children through education.

FRANCINE / RUTH

> Ruth is a mother, a writer, and an artist.

RUTH / JEANNINE
> Jeannine was a nun who won the Chevalier de l'Ordre du Mérite scolaire.

JEANNINE / BARBIE
> Barbie is a writer, a director, and a producer.

ALL
> And here's to all of us.

Dinner Party / Signs of Aging

Violin plays as the women converse and take their seats at the table. Glasses are arranged by RHONDA *and* FRANCINE, *wine poured by* JANICE *and* PAULINE, *and flowers set by* POLLY *and* RUTH.

BARBIE
> Okay, I have a great dinner-party game. I invented this myself. Here's how it works. You go around the table and each person has to mention their most recent sign of aging. Now this has to be a physical sign—the bad stuff, like, "I've begun to choke on my slobber," or "When I wake up in the morning and look in the mirror I look like I've witnessed an automobile accident." Or "I believe I've begun to smell like tinned vegetable soup." There's to be nothing about *empowerment*. It can't be any bullshit like "I seem to have a new sense of self." Okay. Who wants to start? Ruthie?

The Negative Signs of Aging

This is also said/sung to simple, vaudevillian-flavoured piano music.

RUTH
> My bicep used to be on the top, now it's on the bottom.

FRANCINE
> Boxy waist.

JUDY   I'm going bald.

JANICE   Liver spots.

ANN MARIE   I've got a bunion.

GLORIA & CAROLYN
            We think we're shrinking.

LOIS   Chin hair sprouting every morning.

GLENDA   Whoops I'm farting without warning.

PAULINE   I'm gai-ai-ai-ai-ai-ai-ai-ai-ai-ai-ai-ning weight.

POLLY   My face is cracking.

RHONDA   My hands are veiny.

JEANNINE   Decaying body.

BARBIE   And I have a new sense of self!

ALL   Hey!

JANICE   Why is it that we are all so bothered by looking our age, when most of the people in the world would give anything just to *reach* our *age*?

The Invisible Signs of Aging

RUTH   But it's not the visible signs that matter, it's the invisible signs like: becoming my Auntie Sissy with the never-ending litany of people who are sick and dying.

JANICE   I get these unexplained heart spasms.

POLLY   Getting a floater in my eye was extremely scary.

ANN MARIE   My memory is going.

BARBIE   About six years ago I had a hip replacement.

LOIS   I notice I pee when I cough.

PAULINE   Joint pain in da morning.

GLENDA   I can't sleep through the night.

JUDY   I wake up with numb hands.

JOANNA   I'm losing my strength.

FRANCINE   I'm losing my voice to essential tremors.

GLORIA   I notice a more common trait with mules: stubbornness.

RHONDA   Sometimes I am too tired even for sex!

CAROLYN   Only being comfortable in my beloved running shoes.

JEANNINE   Uhhhmmm... Delayed reaction.

GLENDA   What a bunch of whiners. I'm sure that we can say some wonderful things about aging, like those beautiful grandbabies. Just the other day, I was getting ready to take a bubble bath with my granddaughter. She's two, and her mother had just started weaning her off breast milk. So I take off my clothes, and I said, "Come on my girl, take off your diaper." Well she looks up at me, at my breasts, with this look on her face, and I said, "What is it, my girl?" and she says, "K-ook-u-m, I'N SIRSTY."

JANICE   You know what? I love life without tampons.

RUTH   Zetsfleish. It's Yiddish. Literally it means "sitting flesh," you know, that capacity to sit down, focus, and get the job done.

POLLY   Forget about sexy and lacy, I now choose comfortable underwear.

ANN MARIE   I used to care what people say. Now I don't give a shit.

BARBIE   A good thing? Okay. Watching the children you love growing up with a chance of being happy.

LOIS   I'm growing to love my belly.

FRANCINE   You know what? I'm thankful, so thankful, for the scar on my lower abdomen that saw the passage to life of my three adorable children and the scar from my left ear to my neck that permits me today to see, hear, smell, taste, and feel. I'm thankful for this every day.

GLORIA   I'm thankful too. No more mother-in-law.

JOANNA   I am thankful for the friendships that have lasted a lifetime. I used to think, back in the day, you were really old if you had a friend for over twenty years.

RHONDA   I threw the hair dye in the garbage despite my family's objections and decided to go gloriously grey, and I love it.

CAROLYN   And I am thankful for having the health and passion to still do the work I love at seventy-eight… and for… occasionally…

JEANNINE   Reaching wisdom.

ALL   (raising glasses to each other) Occasionally reaching wisdom.

RUTH   And… I have to say, that I am—deeply—thankful… to be alive. When I found out I had cancer I crumbled under a mountain of grief and when I learned I had to have a mastectomy I ceased to function as a wife, as a mother, as a friend. And afterwards, the hole that was left in my chest was mirrored in my soul. I showered with my eyes closed and I looked at the ceiling crying but I never stopped giving thanks for my life.

LOIS   L'chaim!

RUTH   L'chaim!

ALL   To life!

The Bittersweet

FRANCINE Well, we've had the bad and the good and now the bittersweet, like needing my kids more than they need me.

JANICE Losing your parents but not having to be anyone's daughter.

RUTH Despite my horror at having to have a mastectomy, I chose to have a second one. I needed to be sure and I needed to choose.

POLLY I'm free to play golf but, man, I'm tired after the second hole.

ANN MARIE Having my daughter leave home but finally having the bathroom to myself.

BARBIE Finding out that old lovers, the ones you *really* loved, will never leave your heart. But you can't go back.

LOIS I was ravaged by my first hot flash but it was in the middle of winter.

PAULINE Finding the strength to remember me past.

JOANNA I can't sleep as much but I get more done.

GLENDA I was depressed about the kids leaving home, but now Daryl and I have more time together.

CAROLYN I definitely have both hearing loss *and* diminishing eyesight—but only on the right side!

JUDY I am fine on my own but sometimes I long for someone to fall asleep with at the end of the day.

GLORIA It's always nice to be told that my daughters and I could be sisters. But sometimes, I wonder if that means that I look young or that they look older.

JEANNINE I have accepted death but on the other hand I am fearing to die alone.

BARBIE   (*standing up*) Forgive me. If you'll just forgive one little interruption… but I've just this minute come up with a *fantastic* idea. (*to audience*) You know we've all been talking about how great it is to get old. I mean, such a rich experience… I was just kidding about empowerment before. There *is* empowerment and a sense of freedom. And as you can see (*gesturing at other women*) none of us are all upset about starting to look, you know… not so good. I, for example, look forward to looking CRAPPIER WITH EVERY GOD-DAMNED PASSING DAY. So, what about a skin-care line (stay with me) that doesn't make you look younger… but (here's the twist) makes you look *older* even *faster*. You can get in on all the fun… even *earlier*. Like… *right away*. Call the skin-care line something peppy, like "Fast Forward."

          The women get up from the table with their precious item and form into two lines, each pair in a shaft of light.

Precious Items

          Standing in their shafts of light, the women hold their precious objects. Each woman's text slightly overlaps the last.

RUTH   (*holding her Book of Angels*) This is my book of angels. I know, it looks like an address book. When I got sick, I copied down all the names and phone numbers of my friends so my mother and husband could get in touch with all the angels that helped me through. My angels brought endless meals, took care of my children, visited, shopped, called. I don't know how I would have made it without them.

JUDY   (*holding her jade necklace*) My Chinese name, Yook Sum, jade heart. My grandmother gave me this name. When she died, she bequeathed her jade heart to me. It's over one hundred years old.

JEANNINE (*holding her late husband's wedding band*) A fire destroyed almost everything I owned. But two things belonging to my late husband, Yves, were safe. First, a kind of candelabra, and second, his wedding ring. This alliance is always in my middle finger of my right hand.

GLENDA *(holding her father's spittoon)* This was the only possession of my father's that I wanted. His spittoon.

CAROLYN *(holding her mother's red silk jacket)* My mother's red silk jacket… she not only wore this as a maternity garment but throughout her life… it reminds me of her generosity to all and her astonishing courage.

JANICE *(holding her grandmother's po-yas belt)* This belt—po-yas—was woven by the young girl who became my grandmother. It was one of the few possessions she was able to bring from Ukraine to Canada. For me it still holds the touch of her hands and the press of her body.

RHONDA *(holding the book A Tree Grows in Brooklyn)* When I was a little girl my mother worked long hours in a factory. One night, I was about eight, she gave me a book to read, *A Tree Grows in Brooklyn*. I did read it, again and again many times over the years. Today I have seventeen copies in a basket in my living room.

GLORIA *(holding her mother's seeing-eye cane)* This is my mother's seeing-eye cane. She went blind but she never used it. I inherited my mother's glaucoma but I refuse to inherit her pride or her fear.

FRANCINE *(holding her wedding band)* This ring represents twenty-four years of a beautiful family life, a life I finally chose to leave. However, I still cherish cette alliance.

JOANNA *(holding her brother's smudge dish)* This shell is the dish my brother used to burn sweet grass and sage in. My mother gave it to me after he passed away at the tender age of thirty.

PAULINE *(holding her aunt's wooden spoon)* This is my Aunt Stella's spoon, the aunt who rescued me. She used it to mix lemonade and that's the only thing I have to remember her by.

LOIS *(holding her father's sweater)* I have my father's sense of humour, the twinkle in his eye, and his head with numbers. And his sweater. My dad was a salesman and he had to wear a suit most days. But on Sundays, he liked to wear this sweater.

43

ANN MARIE   (*holding her grandmother's gold earrings*) This is a pair of gold earrings that my grandmother, who was really my mother, left me when she died. When I hold them in my hands I can feel her next to me.

POLLY   (*holding her daughter's gold bracelets*) Because of an estrangement from my family, my daughter did not receive the traditional gift of gold bracelets. When my sister died she passed on this pair, given to her son, for my baby. They were a gift of love, welcoming us back into the family.

BARBIE   There has never been anything to me more precious than David Kenneth Cole. We never married. We never had children, but we were as close as two people can be for over thirty years. He died almost exactly two years ago at sixty-two. Heart attack. Dropped like a stone and gone. (*holds out empty hands*) And gone for good.

The women turn to the right and stand with their backs to the audience.

Rants

With their backs to the audience, each woman turns to the front to deliver her rant. When she finishes she returns to face the back.

JANICE   One of the greatest gifts of aging is that we're ready to face the deep and dark things in life, and that we're ready to show something men have always owned: anger. Not bad temper, but anger that cuts to the quick of what's wrong with the world and lights the way for us to change things. What we may lose in smooth skin and taut bellies we more than make up for with our power to blaze up in clear, bright anger.

RHONDA   I dare anyone to go to a pharmacy tonight and buy a set of earplugs. I dare you to wear them for an hour and see what it's like for me to hear you. See what it's like when someone talks with their hands over their mouths. When their hair falls to cover half of their face. When my eyes strain to capture the punchline of a good joke. I dare you to see what it's like not to have what most of you take for granted, every time you hear a story, listen to music, watch a play, or have a conversation in a darkened room. I am trying to hear you. Are you listening?

POLLY   I was mercilessly beaten by my two older brothers in our driveway. My mother was screaming, "Stop you'll kill her." She knew that if my father was alive, he would have got out his gun. Why? Because I was in love. He was black and we are Indian.

RUTH   In the last four years I've had five operations, eight rounds of chemo, written a book, secured a publishing contract, cooked and served one thousand nine hundred and eighty-six meals, and done twelve thousand loads of laundry. So yes, I do work!

ANN MARIE In my first job in this country, one day before a lavish party, my employer proudly showed me her new hat. The hat cost $650. My salary? One hundred and twenty-five dollars a week. And shall I tell you about the behaviour of the man of the house?

FRANCINE   Don't tell me what I'm thinking. Stop deciding what's in my head, you don't know. Let me talk, listen.

JOANNA   My grandparents had all their children taken from them and put into an Indian residential school. Both my parents spent their entire youth in these schools, where they experienced physical, sexual, and psychological abuse. Especially my father. He went in an innocent child and came out a man full of rage. I witnessed this rage and I inherited that rage. I'm pissed off that we have the highest incarceration rate, the highest infant mortality rate, the highest suicide rate. And I'm disappointed that many Canadians don't make the connection.

GLORIA   What makes me so furious
           The men a.k.a. boys.
           Pushing their music videos
           With hip-shaking
           Booty-showing
           Butt-naked
           Women a.k.a. girls
           Dancing to a beat
           That leaves me
           Cold

Unfeeling
Without heat
Porno TV
Creating a world
That
My grandbabies
Need not see.

BARBIE   Here's what pisses me off: Religion. And by religion, I mean everything from the tippy-top of the church right down to crystals. But even *I'm* not immune. A couple of years ago I was diagnosed with cancer. This calls up all sorts of questions. Not "Why me?" because why the hell *not* me? But questions like "Why did it happen?" "How did it happen?" Unanswerable questions. But I came up with an answer that, I think, makes as much sense as anything else. Jesus gave me cancer… to get back at me… for being confirmed in my tennis dress.

CAROLYN   My grandmother, mother, aunt, and late ex-husband were all tormented alcoholics. I lived for so long with the feeling of helplessness and dread—and I look back with sadness and profound anger at the wreckage of these precious lives.

JUDY   I am a widow and no one seems to get it. Don't tell me "He's in a better place." Apparently that means that life here on earth with me and the kids must have really sucked. The death of someone you love is not something you get over.

GLENDA   I know a woman named Sylvia. She was raped by three men. And when she tried to fight back, they beat her unconscious. She told me the police said there was really nothing they could do, but I believe it was because she was a heroin addict, because she was poor, and because she was a woman.

JEANNINE   Je suis enragée at the church for the rape of my conscience.

LOIS   My best friend was forbidden by her husband to step into my house or introduce me to her child. When my seven-year-old son proudly told the teacher that he had a new sister, he was called a liar in front of his grade-one class. I know of a judge who thought it was best to give a child to his abusive father rather than his dyke mom. What is so scary about a woman loving another woman?

PAULINE walks between the women.

PAULINE   I'm angry at my father for leaving us with my aunt and uncle. I'm angry my aunt for beatin' us for everything. I'm angry at them for not sending us to school. I'm angry at my uncle for busting my sister's head with the cow chain and set the dog after her when she run. Most of all I'm angry for my mother for not coming back to get us.

> *As she sings her song, PAULINE eventually makes her way to her knees, downstage centre. The women are drawn into her, connecting and comforting each other.*

Two little sisters were walking one day, down by the dark riverside, They were singing and shouting and praising the Lord; the Lord will provide.
Two little sisters were walking one day, down by the dark riverside, They were singing and shouting and praising the Lord; the Lord will provide.
The Lord will provide. The Lord will provide. The Lord... will... provide.

The Soul

JEANNINE   Although the soul is invisible, it can touch others, and it can be touched by others.

> *All walk into a line downstage and sit on the floor.*

Death

Sitting on the floor in a straight line across downstage, each woman lies down after finishing her story.

LOIS   I can remember really clearly the first time I knew I was going to die. I was fourteen years old, working at my first summer job, and I wanted the day to be over. I looked up. The clock said 4:00 but I knew that 5:00 was coming. And it was going to come tomorrow. Five o'clock would be there every day and one day I would die.

BARBIE   There have been five deaths that really broke my heart. My mother; my childhood friend Johnnie, who died in my arms; two little dogs: Sporty and Pinky; and David. I treasure the truth that in each and every case my last words to them were "I love you." I love you, Mummy. I love you, Johnnie. I love you, Sporty. I love you, Pinky.

I love you, David.

POLLY   With my father's death the Brahmin ways of our family started to slip away. His children married outside of our caste, religion, and race.

RHONDA   I hadn't seen my father in twelve or thirteen years. One night I had a dream that he appeared at my wedding. I was so happy. I asked if we could stay in touch and he said no. I turned away, and when I looked back he was gone. Two weeks later I got a letter saying that he had died that weekend.

PAULINE   When I was younger I thought that if I died, I would be happier.

GLENDA   My beautiful sister was an addict on Skid Row. Her life… it was unimaginable. One night my beautiful sister was sitting at a bar when a tall, skinny bald man that everybody knew came up to her and said, "You wanna party?" My sister said, "Sure." And she hopped into his car. They started driving and she asked him, "Where are we going?" He said, "To my farm in Poco." She said, "Well, I don't want to go that far for a party." She had a feeling, so while the car was still moving she jumped out and ran back to the bar. That man was Robert Pickton.

JUDY   When Andrew was sick lying in his bed, he had become unrecognizable from the cancer. I looked at him and said, "Andrew you are beautiful." "What do you mean, I can't move, I can't provide, I can't do anything." But what is left is the real pure you.

JOANNA I died when I was twelve years old. It was a rainy Friday night and I was crossing the street with my arms full of pop bottles when I was hit by car, and I died. In the ambulance I could hear my grandfather, who had long since been deceased, singing me old Indian songs, bringing me back to life.

JANICE I can't stop thinking of that girl in my grandmother's village, the one who hanged herself from the rafters of her father's barn because her family forbade her to marry for love. How she lay in her open coffin with her long, thick braid wrapped round and round her neck to hide the bruises made by the rope.

GLORIA When I was a young girl I had a good friend who always seemed to have spare pennies and often lent me some so that I could buy cookies from the teacher. One day on his way home from school he was killed for those few pennies he had in his pocket. All the kids told me that if someone dies and you owe them money, their spirit would come back to collect. At his funeral, mixed with my sorrow was this fear that he really would come back. So, when no one was looking I secretly placed three pennies in his coffin.

RUTH   I have faced my own mortality. Despite the inevitability of death, when it comes to me or those that I love, I will be shocked and outraged and grief-stricken.

ANN MARIE My mamasita's death hit me like a hammer, but I feel her in here.

CAROLYN Recently, a beloved architect friend, knowing her cancer was inoperable and little time was left, said to me: "Carolyn, I can walk around this city and see buildings I have created; I have loved and I have been loved, what more can I ask?" Her funeral was in January. Her words unforgettable. I have no fear of death.

JEANNINE Well, I am not in a hurry. Je voudrais vivre jusqu'a deux cents ans. I want to live to be two hundred.

FRANCINE   When my mother died the undertaker suggested an avocado green coffin. It was the fashionable colour at the time. Mathieu, Katherine, Sébastien, a cardboard box will be just fine.

Extros

All stand up one by one when it is their turn to speak; they are assisted up by the previous speaker, to violin music that suggests joyful triumph.

LOIS   Four years ago me and my dyke posse challenged the antiquated laws of the Ontario government and now we don't have to adopt our own children.

BARBIE   The funny thing is… for some reason, cancer lifted my depression. Maybe it was because I had a tangible enemy to fight. I don't know. But having said that I feel I should caution you that cancer used as an antidepressant can have some *very* serious side effects.

POLLY   My daughter is free to marry anyone she chooses, or not. If they are happy together, I will be overjoyed.

JOANNA   I lived with my inherited rage and it affected everyone around me, especially those I love, until I finally understood where that rage came from and I was able to transform it into positive action, action that I will continue for the rest of my days.

PAULINE   I come from having no shoes and being kept home from school to earning my doctorate in cosmetology, owning two hair salons, and I have hundreds of beautiful shoes.

GLENDA   After many years of not knowing myself I was finally awakened. Now, I am able to serve those who really need me: women like Sylvia, and my own mother, my beautiful sister, and thousands of other beautiful forgotten souls.

JUDY   When my husband died, my children and I were shattered. But now I know he lives, I see him in them every day.

JANICE   I have found my face; I have fashioned a face for myself out of love, not hate.

GLORIA   My revolutionary name was Ochumi, now it's Oma.

RUTH   When we first started working on the show, my line was "I'm done giving away body parts." Recently I had to relinquish some more to the surgeon's scalpel. Now I'm really done giving away body parts.

ANN MARIE   I always longed for a mother's love. Now I have become the mother I never had.

FRANCINE   Although I am haunted by my childhood sexual abuse, it will not defeat me. I am proud to say I teach children everywhere that they have rights, especially the right to say no.

CAROLYN   At seventy-eight I am ready for more exploration and adventure in the theatre. It turned out that my devastating onstage stroke sixteen years ago, was, for me, a stroke of luck.

JEANNINE   Je suis toujours Jeannine, I will be eighty in July. Not afraid anymore.

RHONDA   I now have a second cochlear implant and I thought my favourite sound was the sound of seeds from a sweet pepper falling into a sink. My new favourite sound is fourteen women laughing.

ALL   *(laugh)*

> *The women raise their hands to the sky.* PAULINE *sings the traditional song from Act One.*

PAULINE   A chi chi bod ho!
Suma dem a halla suma ball
Suma black bird
Suma dem a halla suma a ball
Suma Chi chi
Suma dem a halla suma a ball

ALL   A chi chi bad ho! Suma them a halla suma ball

PAULINE   Suma black bird

ALL   Suma dem a halla suma ball

PAULINE   Suma Chi Chi

ALL   Suma dem a halla suma ball

PAULINE   A Chi Chi bod ho

ALL   Suma dem a halla suma ball

Fin.

Acknowledgements

This play would not have been possible without the blessing and support of Geoff Craig, the Unilever folks Sharon MacLeod and Margaret McKellar, and Brenda Surminski and Janet Kestin at Ogilvy & Mather. I would like to thank all of the amazing women who wrote letters, who auditioned, and who made up our phenomenal audience. The second and third productions of this play only happened because of the extraordinary drive and passion of Lois Fine and Brenda Surminski (working independently), I went along for the ride. Most of us worked for the love of the piece, as there was little to no money available, but the play was 100% sold out for all three productions, which meant there was actually some revenue for the company of women to share at the end. But this was gravy; although there were naturally some difficulties along the way, we were all passionate about this project.

Biographies

Joanna Anaquod, 54, a Saulteaux from Saskatchewan, has been relentless in campaigning to raise awareness of First Nations rights and issues since appearing on a *Toronto Life* cover at 18. The child of parents that attended Indian residential schools, she has an intimate understanding of how multi-generational grief is passed on in an adverse manner. Through her own grief and rage, she grew to understand that her parents were not at fault, but rather the paternalistic and colonial legislation of the Crown in their attempt to "get the Indian out of the Indian" while ignoring the treaties and Indian rights. Today, Joanna works for an all-Native law firm; she also works with her three daughters in film, television, and music videos, and helps with their many Aboriginal youth initiatives. Downtime is celebrating time with her new granddaughter Willow Rose, being anywhere on the land, taking long walks with her dog Mukwa, dancing the night away, or spending treasured quiet time with friends and family. Joanna resides in Orillia with her husband Russell, a Mohawk from Kanawake.

Jeannine Boucher, 80, was born in Montreal during the Depression of 1929. A widowed and retired special-education teacher and administrator, Jeannine eventually found the strength to overcome her challenges. She is an optimist and focuses on the privileges of being old. Jeannine is curious and her major interests are theology, philosophy, psychology, literature, theatre, and concerts. She also writes poetry and creates visual art. She appreciated getting to work with Judith Thompson in her first collective creation, this adventure of *Body*

JUDITH THOMPSON

& Soul. Lastly, Jeannine found a new "dada" haiku—after thirty-three days in a monastery (thirty days in silence).

Polly Clarke was born into a Trinidadian family of twelve, of East Indian descent, and raised as a Hindu, and describes herself as a cultural "chameleon." Through her travels in Europe and Asia, Polly has developed a wonderful ability to blend in and adapt to other cultures. Now retired, she was a high-school English teacher and a Leader for Heritage Education in North York. Polly believes yoga and the occasional game of golf keep her young, and despite worrying that she is too timid on stage, knows she can rely on the wisdom and strength of her fellow cast members.

Lois Fine grew up in Montreal and moved to Toronto at nineteen, but she still believes Montreal bagels are the best. Lois is a CGA and director of finance in the charities sector. She is also a performer/writer/singer/songwriter, and very recently a producer. She has two beautiful children who she looks up to in every way, and is grateful for the love in her life.

Francine Robert-Grainger has dedicated much of her life to education, helping children and youth find their strengths and dreams, and has inspired them to pursue those dreams. Retired from the French school board, she is now working as a consultant for le Centre ontarien de prévention des agressions, offering workshops and producing documentaries on bullying, sexism, homophobia, and racism. She is the proud mother of three artistic children and the grandmother of two little angels. By letting her inner child play with the woman she has become, she lives her life to the fullest by transforming her passions into realities.

At 5'11", Ann Marie Hasley stands tall and proud, but it wasn't always so. Growing up in Trinidad, she was not-so-affectionately referred to by others as a "giraffe" and made to feel ugly. She attributes her resilience to her grandmother, who raised her to be the strong and independent woman she is today. She has passed those same traits on to her three wonderful children. As a social worker who has dedicated most of her career to autistic children, Ann Marie has acted as a mother figure to many more.

Carolyn Hetherington is an award-winning actor who has worked in theatre, film, and television in Canada, England, Scotland, and Australia for the last forty years. Theatre highlights include Necessary Angel's *Half Life*, Stratford's *Henry VIII*, the Centaur and Citadel's *The Beauty Queen of Leenane*, *Wit* at the Centaur and GCTC, and many others including the amazing *Body & Soul*.

Her work in film and television includes Sarah Polley's *Away From Her*, *Blue Murder*, *Anne of Avonlea*, and *Anne of Green Gables* to name a few. Carolyn and her partner Douglas share seven children and thirteen grandchildren and live happily on a lake near Kingston.

Glenda Klassen (Delorme), 56, was born into a Cree First Nation tribe. Second oldest of eight girls and one boy, Glenda's youth was one of survival—survival from a generation of residential school parents. Plagued by alcoholism, abandonment, and loss Glenda learned to conquer the coerced and callous life of two generations. Today she journeys through life with her husband Darryl, six children, and ten grandchildren. Glenda works toward helping to restore and revive a stolen culture for her family and other Aboriginal women. All My Relations!

Janice Kulyk Keefer is the author of numerous works of poetry, fiction, and creative non-fiction. She lives in Toronto and teaches English and creative writing at the University of Guelph. Her latest novel is *The Ladies' Lending Library*, published by Harper Collins Canada.

Barbara Nichol, 55, has been a news writer, television and radio comedy writer, documentary maker for CBC's Radio's *Ideas*, and producer and author of their April 1 hoaxes and various radio plays. She is the author of six books and other works for children (including the original recording of *Beethoven Lives Upstairs*). Barbara wrote the film *Home For Blind Women*, which won the Genie for best short film, and has been a contributing editor at *The Walrus*. She began as a comic essayist and has returned to her roots with a humour column for the online magazine Adinfinitummag.com.

Pauline Patten was born in Jamaica to a mother who left when she was a baby. Under the care of a great aunt, she was subjected to abuse and long days in the fields. She got by on the hope that her mother would one day come rescue her. When it didn't happen, Pauline still managed to find forgiveness. Pauline's strength and resilience have helped her get where she is today. She now owns a hair salon in Halifax and is a chronic giver to the community. *Body & Soul* has given her the chance to help women see that we all have struggles.

Ruth Rakoff leads a busy life raising three boys. She has had an eclectic career path including stints as a cook, a daycare director, and a family mediator. Ruth has dabbled in a variety of art forms and with *Body & Soul* she adds theatre to her repertoire, taking on a lifetime of stage fright. Her first book, a memoir entitled *When My World Was Very Small* will be published in September 2010 by Random House.

Gloria Schmed-Scott, 65, was born in Brooklyn, New York, to a very protective mother and father who never let her stray beyond the viewpoint of their front window. Her whole world fit between two fire hydrants until her mother sent her to live with an aunt and uncle in the Deep South. Here, racism and segregation would groom her for the civil rights movement, sit-ins, even a brief jail stay. Now, as a senior, she hopes to persuade older women not to settle for invisibility, a challenge she first took on in her days as an activist.

Rhonda Tepper, 51, is a parent and teacher living in Toronto. Before collaborating on *Body & Soul* she was and continues to be active in the Stagecraft Theatre Company. She has performed for Luminato and in a video about accessibility for the Toronto District School Board. Rhonda has lived in New Brunswick; Thunder Bay, Ontario; Lyon, France; and Montreal, Quebec. She continues to grow and to enjoy her ongoing passions for everything Italian, the Maritime provinces, Leonard Cohen, and New York City. Her favourite word is "wonder."

Judith Thompson is a playwright, director, screenwriter, actor, and teacher of theatre, and is a two-time winner of the Governor General's Literary Award for *White Biting Dog* and *The Other Side of the Dark*. She has been invested as an Officer in the Order of Canada, was awarded the prestigious Susan Smith Blackburn Prize for her play *Palace of the End* in 2008, and won the 2009 Amnesty International Freedom of Expression Award for the same play. Judith is a professor of drama at the University of Guelph and lives with her husband and five children in Toronto.

Judy Wark has lived and worked in Kenya, Hong Kong, Belize, Australia, and now Canada. After losing her young husband to melanoma, she wound her way through grief and loss to create the second act of her life in Calgary. She is a mother, writer, motivational speaker, and communications coordinator for Hospice Calgary.